"Exploring the Earth and Beyond"
Funding for this item provided by a
Library Services and Technology (LSTA)
Grant made possible by the Illinois
State Library - 2013

Grasshoppers

Siân Smith

Raintree

Chicago, Illinois

www.capstonepub.com
Visit our website to find out more information about Heinemann-Raintree books.

To order:

☎ Phone 800-747-4992

💻 Visit www.capstonepub.com to browse our catalog and order online.

Edited by Dan Nunn, Rebecca Rissman, and Sian Smith
Designed by Joanna Hinton-Malivoire
Picture research by Ruth Blair
Originated by Capstone Global Library Ltd
Production by Victoria Fitzgerald
Printed in China by South China Printing Company Ltd

16 15 14 13 12
10 9 8 7 6 5 4 3 2 1

Library of Congress Cataloging-in-Publication Data
Smith, Siân.
  Grasshoppers / Sian Smith.
    p. cm.—(Creepy critters)
  Includes bibliographical references and index.
  ISBN 978-1-4109-4808-3 (hb)—ISBN 978-1-4109-4821-2 (pb) 1.
  Grasshoppers—Juvenile literature. I. Title.
  QL508.A2S63 2013
  595.7'26—dc23   2011041229

Acknowledgments
We would like to thank the following for permission to reproduce photographs: Dreamstime.com pp.8 (© Photomyeye), 9 (© Vaughan Jessnitz), 13, 23 (© Marispro), 17 (© Eva-christiane Wilm), 22, 22 (© Aetmeister), 22 (© Biansho), 22 (© Kodo34), 23 (© Giuliano2022), 23 (© Petrp), 23 (© Martin Valigursky), 23 (© Alexey Fedorov); iStockphoto pp.15 (© Antagain), 16 (© Alexander Shams); Naturepl p.18 (© Paul Harcourt Davies); Photoshot p.21 (© NHPA); Shutterstock pp.5 (© Tyler Fox), 6 (© Ingrid Prats), 6 (© kurt_G), 7 (© Dirk Ercken), 7 (© Marek R. Swadzba), 7 (© Anke van Wyk), 11 (© Denis Vesely), 12 (© ded pixto), 14 (© USBFCO), 15 (© Rob McKay), 15 (© Jason Steel), 19 (© Hway Kiong Lim), 23 (© Leighton Photography & Imaging).

Front cover photograph reproduced with permission of Shutterstock (© Jonas Kvist Jensen).

The publisher would like to thank Michael Bright for his help in the preparation of this book.

Every effort has been made to contact copyright holders of any material reproduced in this book. Any omissions will be rectified in subsequent printings if notice is given to the publisher.

Contents

Strange Sounds

Can you hear that strange noise?
What's making the sound?

Somewhere on this page
there's a creepy critter around!

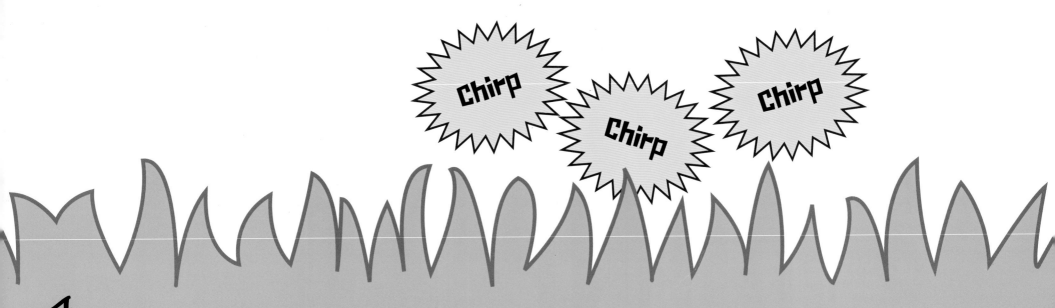

Meet a Grasshopper

The sound comes from a grasshopper, but there are many different sorts.

Some are green and some are brown.
Their feelers are long or short.

short feelers

long feelers

7

Feelers are called antennae.
A grasshopper uses them to smell.

Antennae are amazing things!
They can pick up movement as well.

antennae

Grasshoppers don't have ears like you,
so they won't hear you saying please.

Some do have parts that work like ears,
a bit below their knees.

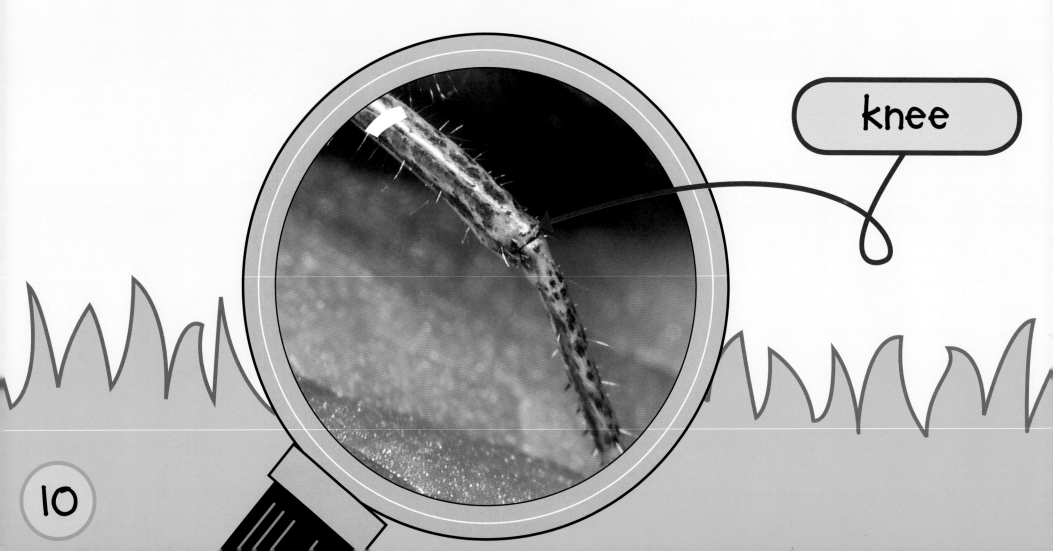

knee

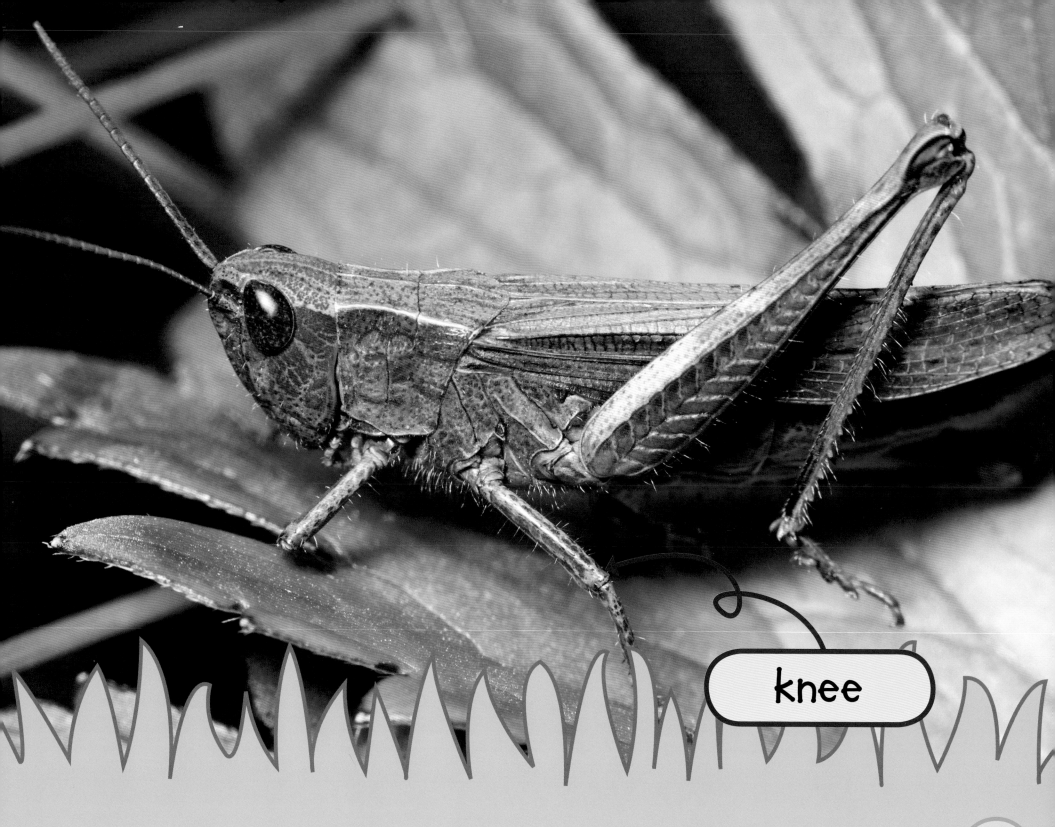

knee

How many legs does a grasshopper have? Can you count them all?

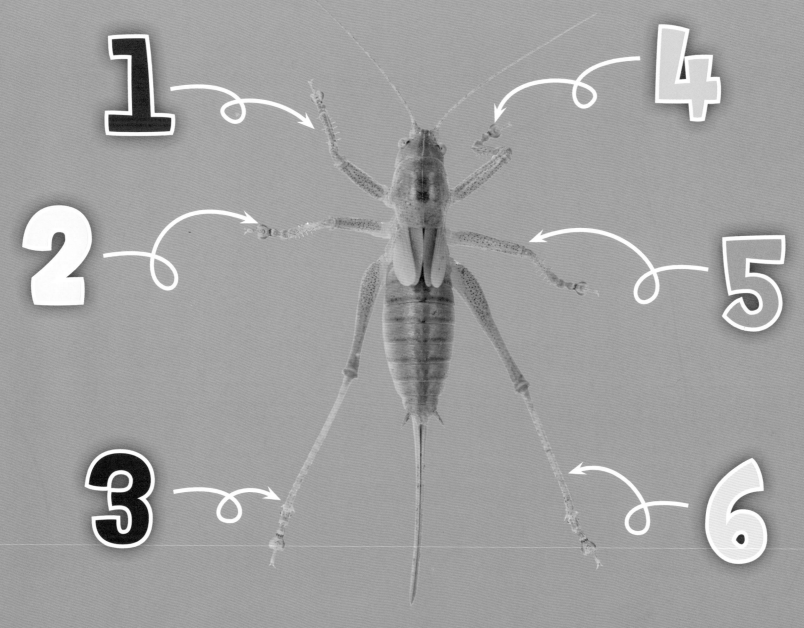

A grasshopper has two huge back legs,
and four at the front that are small.

Jumpers and Fliers

Grasshoppers are amazing jumpers. They often jump to escape!

Many animals like to eat them,
such as birds, frogs, toads, and snakes.

Most grasshoppers cannot fly.
They use their wings to glide.

wing

But locusts are grasshoppers
that fly to eat plants far
and wide.

Tiny Babies

Baby grasshoppers are born in eggs.
They hatch out in the spring.

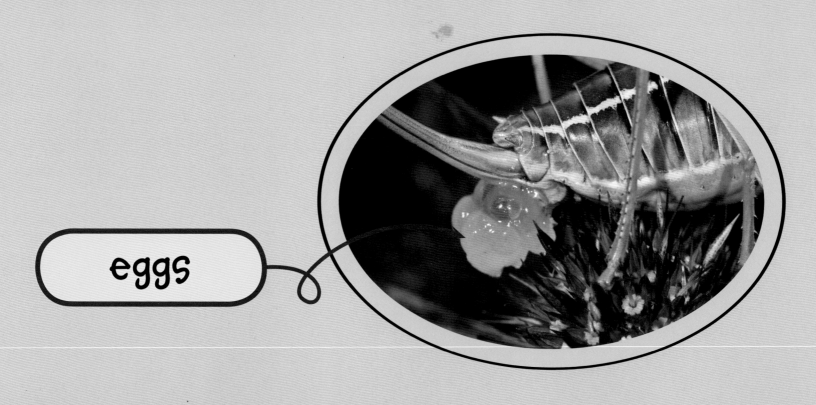

eggs

Young grasshoppers can be tiny.
They look like adults without wings.

Grasshopper Music

Male grasshoppers are often noisy, but do you know how they sing?

Some grasshoppers make their wings go "crack." Others rub a foot on a wing.

Hunt the Hoppers

How many grasshoppers are there here?
Make sure you take a good look.

To find out whether you were right, turn around this page of the book.

Answer: ten grasshoppers.

23

Did You Know?

Grasshoppers have hooks on their feet so that they can hold onto plants.

Index

24